If I Grow Silent

If Our Paths Don't Cross Again

Death Interrupted

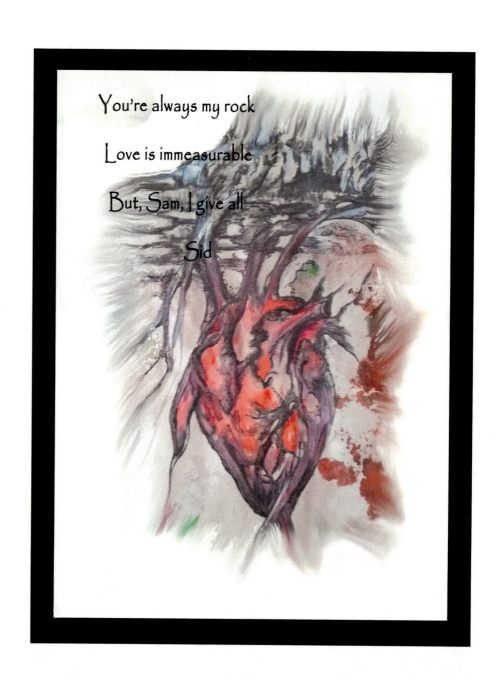

Calicified Abode
Undetered Journeyman
Where Are You Rushing
Susan

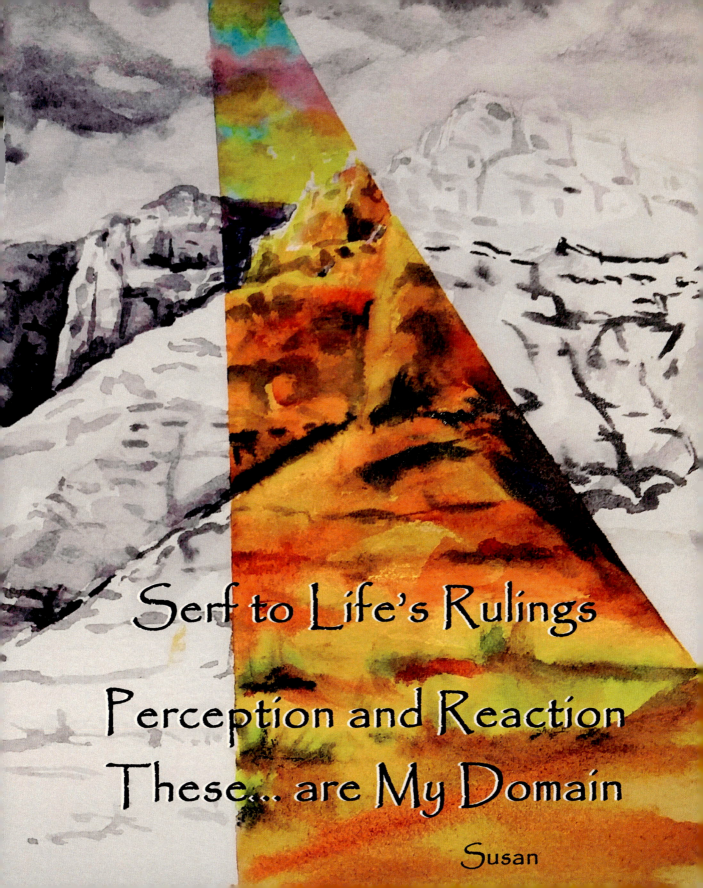

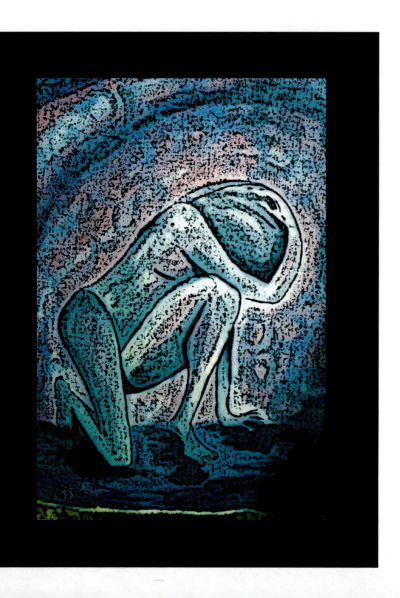

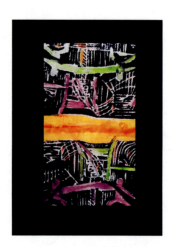

Closed Eyes, Heart Opened

Receptive to Sounds Around

Earth's Symphony Plays

Susan

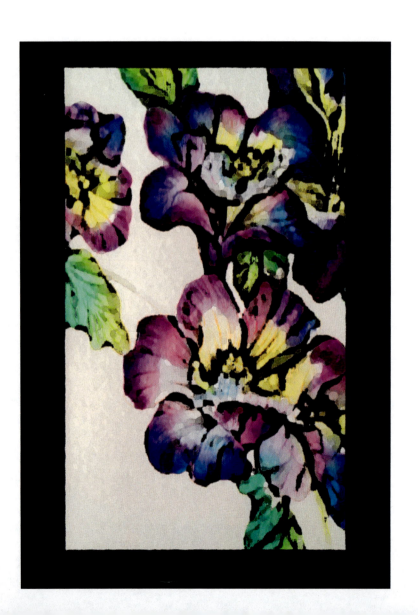

Kissed by a Stranger

Wings Pulsing While We Embrace

Unconditional

Susan

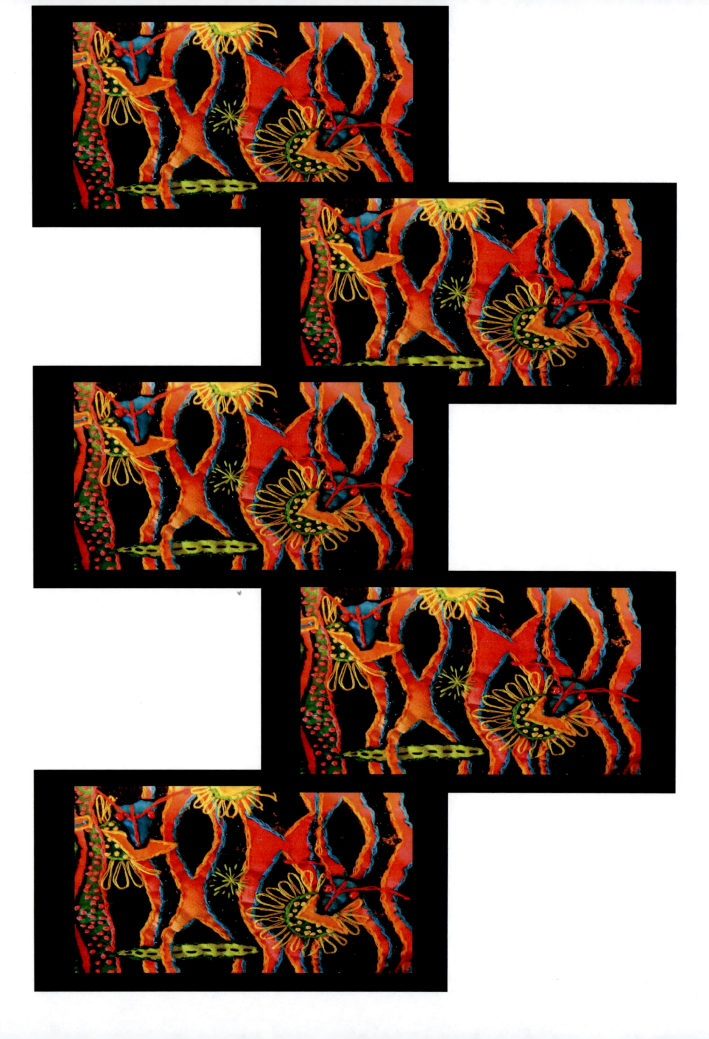

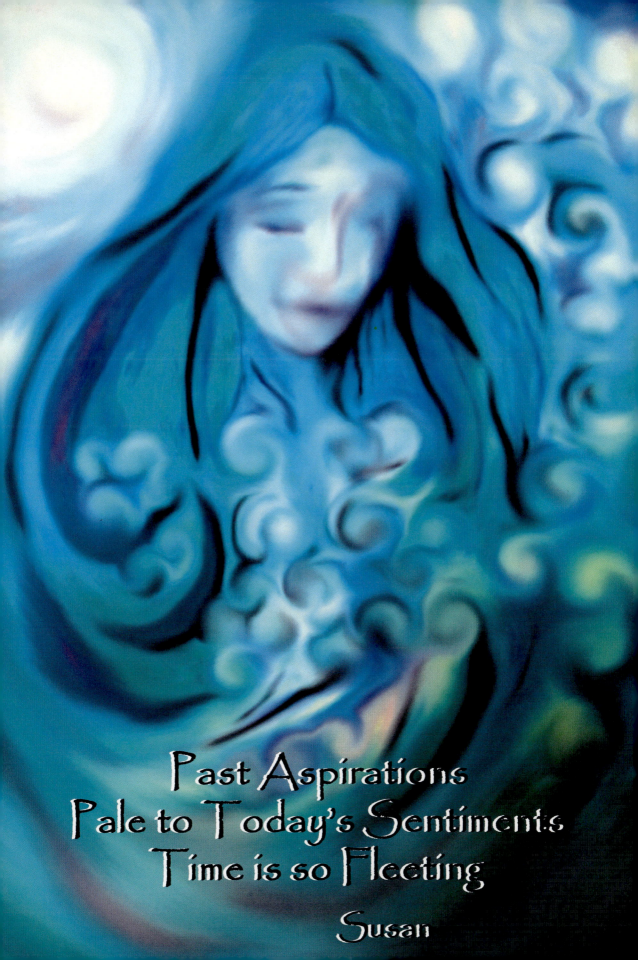

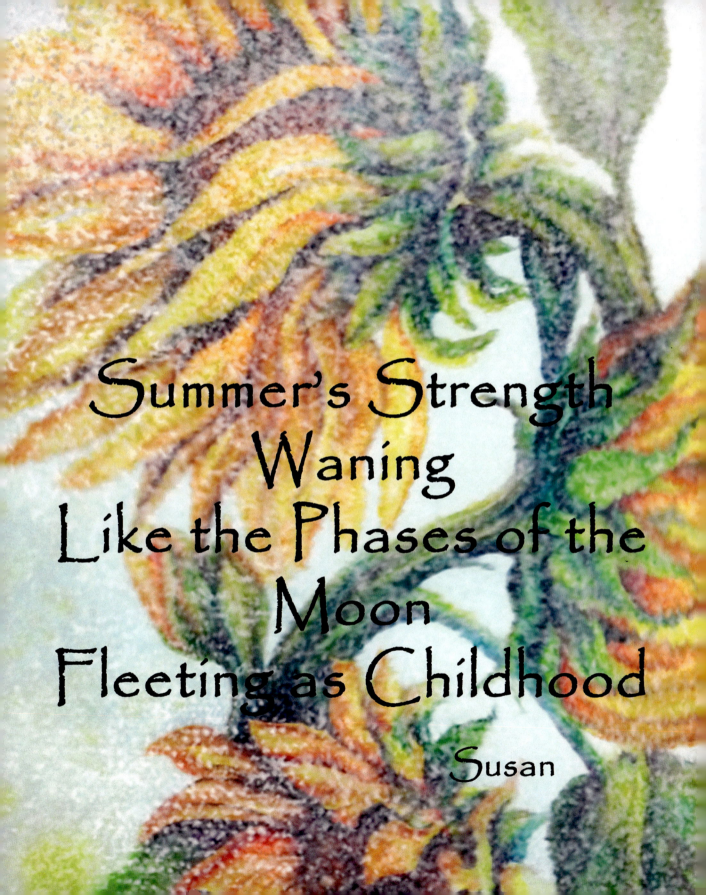

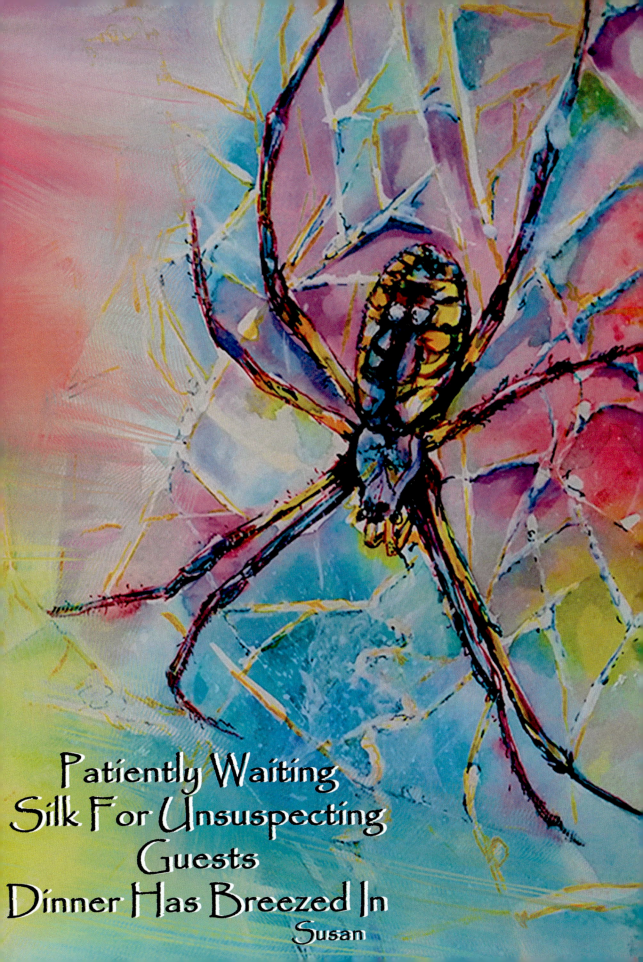

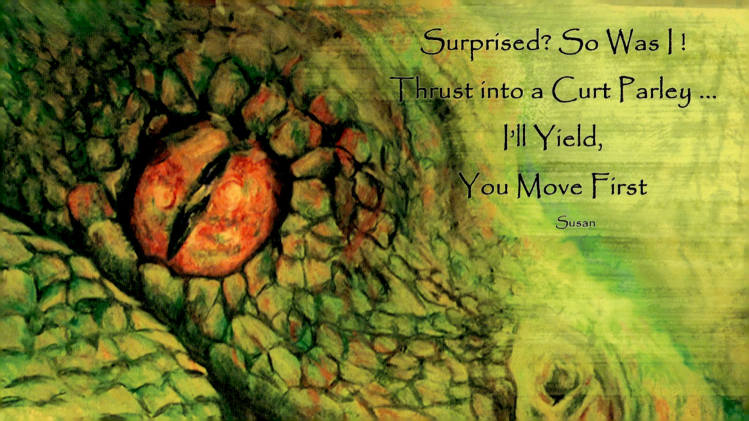

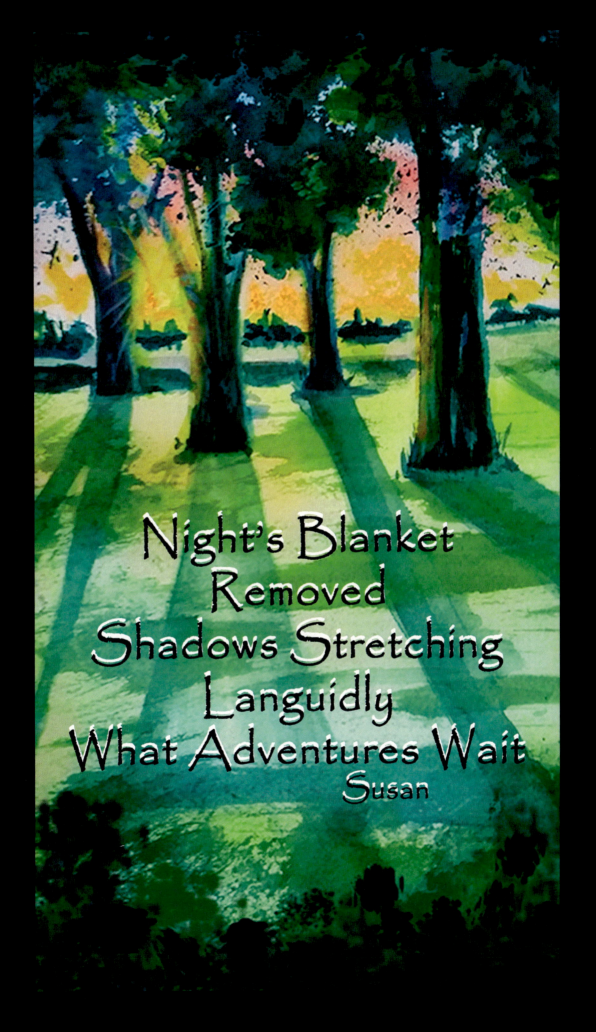

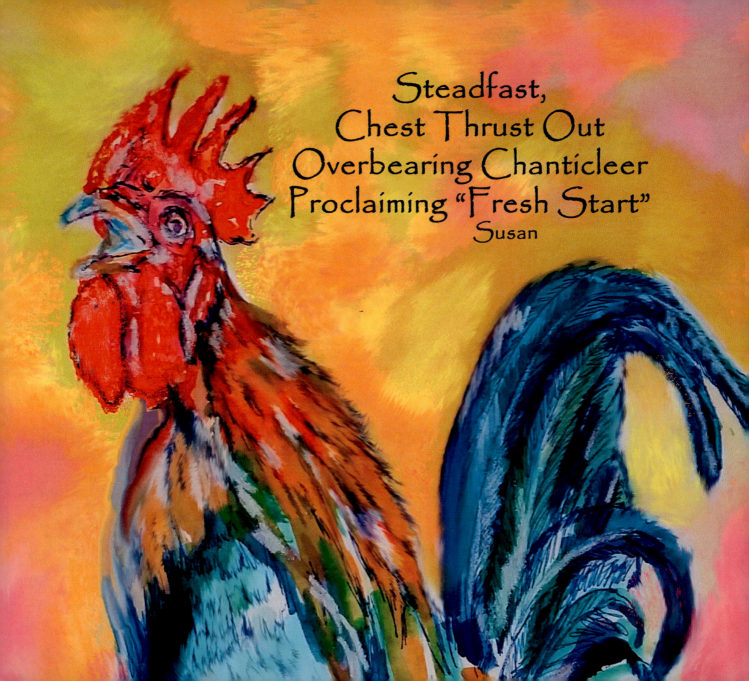

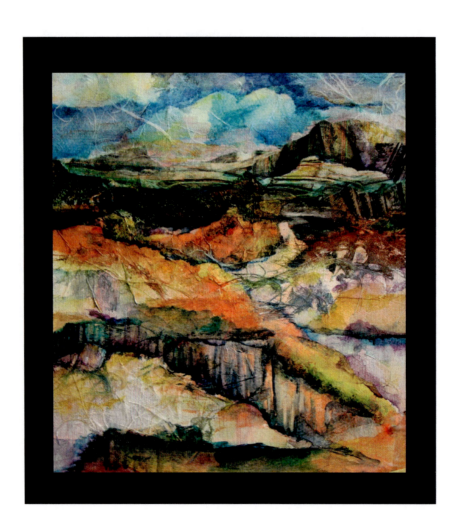

Watercolor

Quenching the Parched Ground

Each Living Organism

Submerged in Lifeblood

Susan

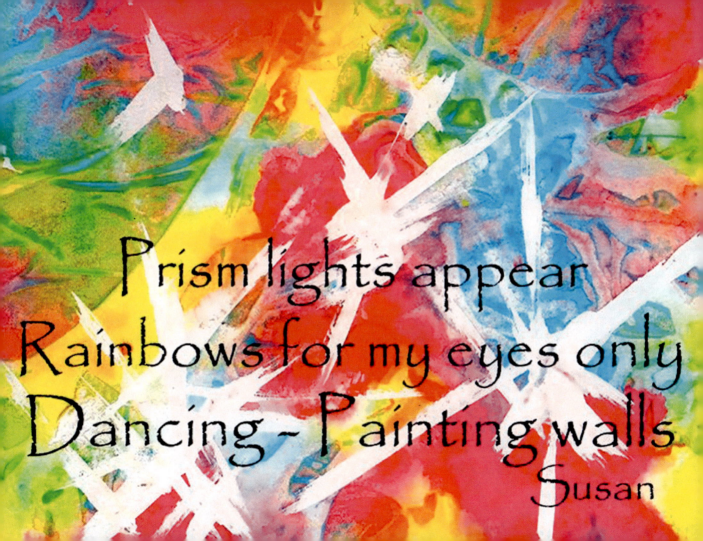

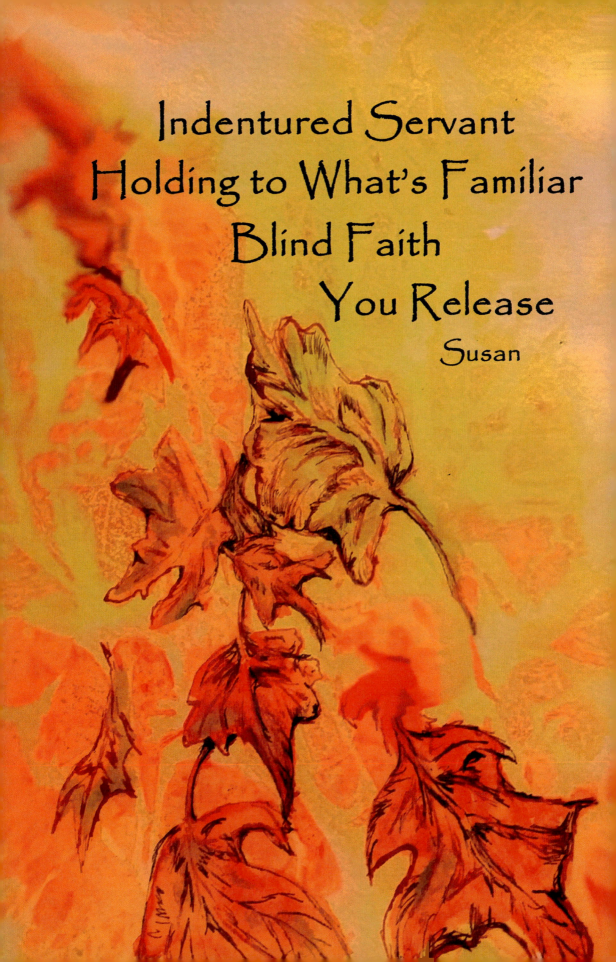

Indentured Servant
Holding to What's Familiar
Blind Faith
You Release
Susan

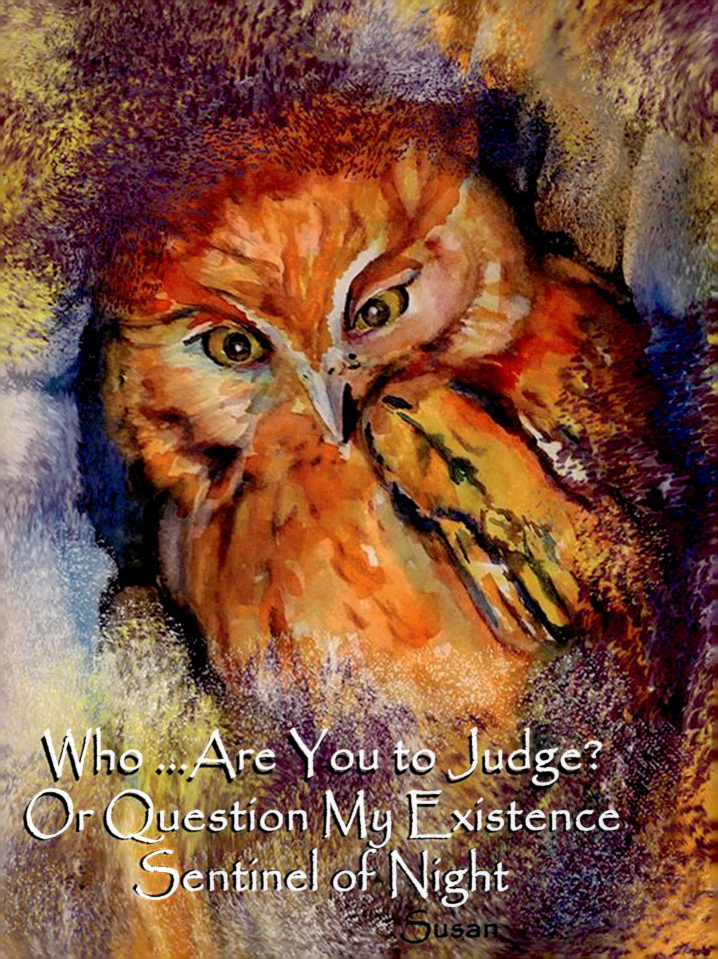

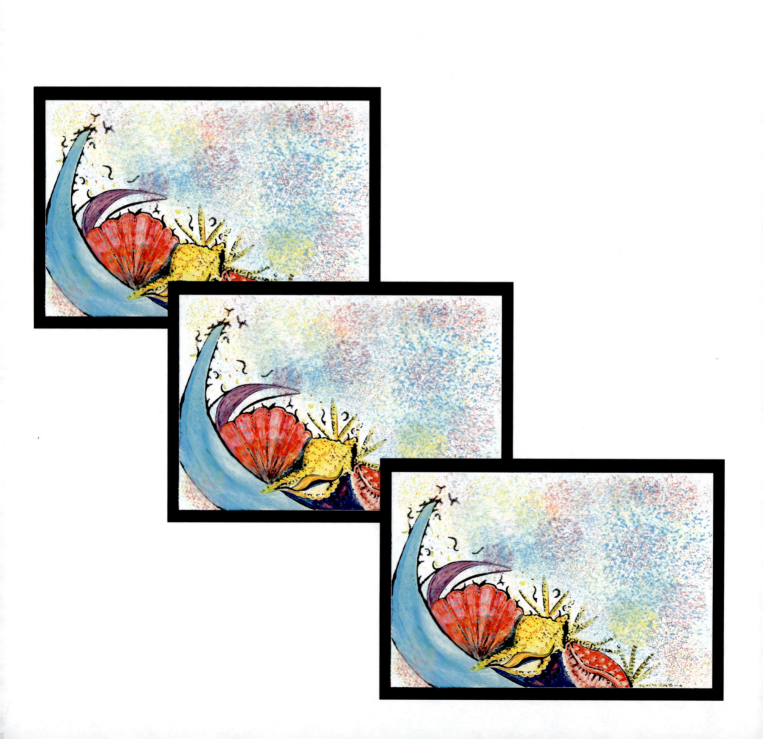

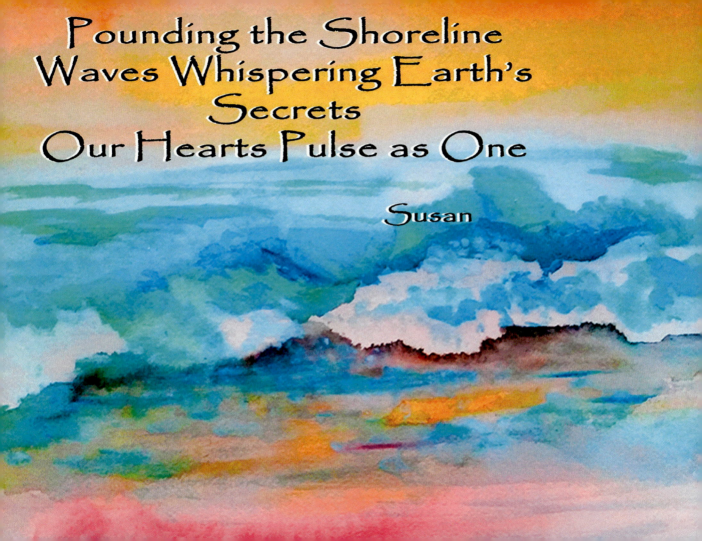

First Light, Tranquillo
A Cappella Crescendos
Nature's Sonata

Susan

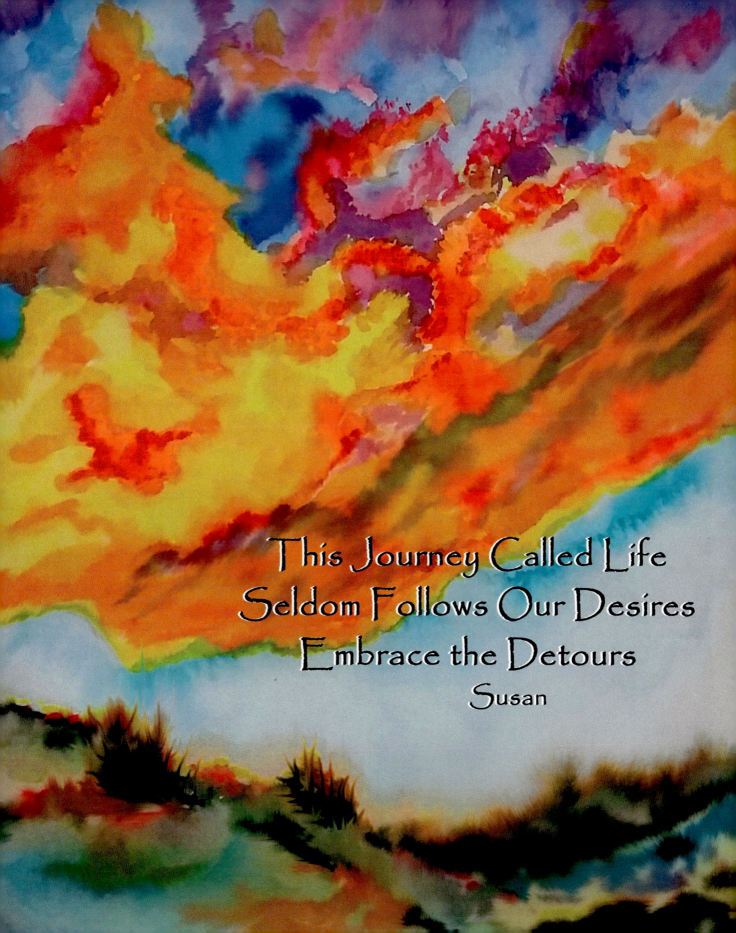

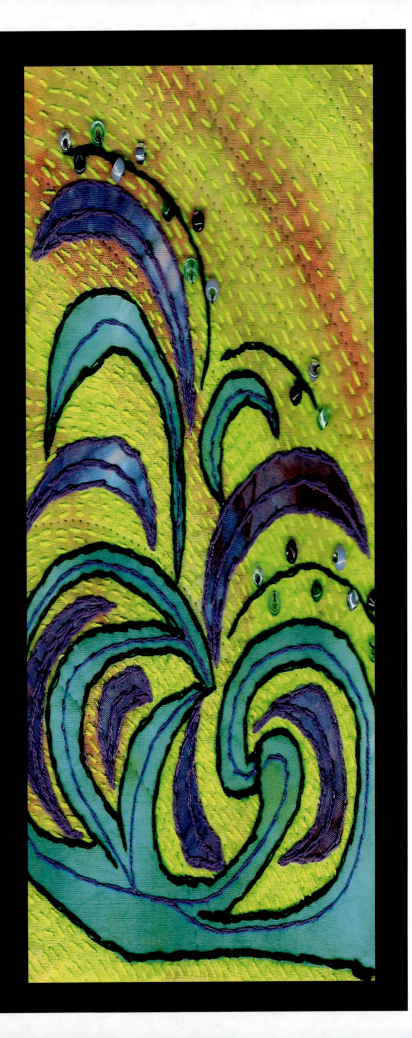

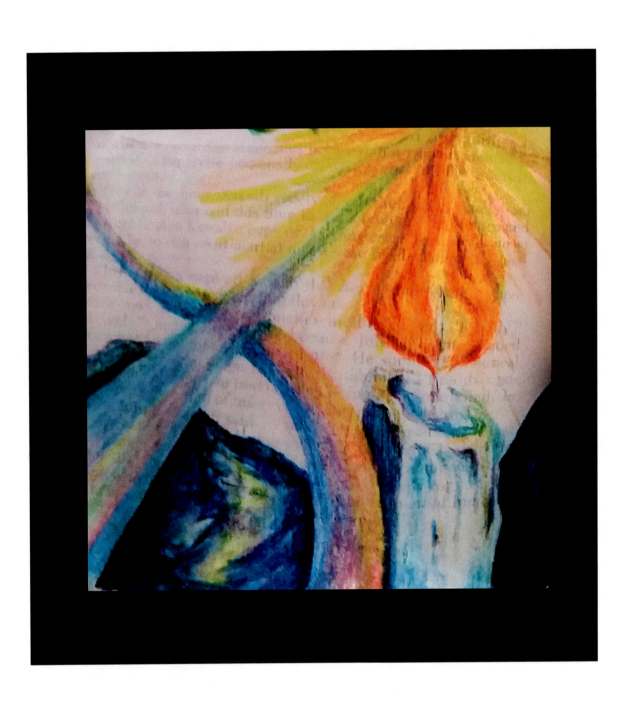

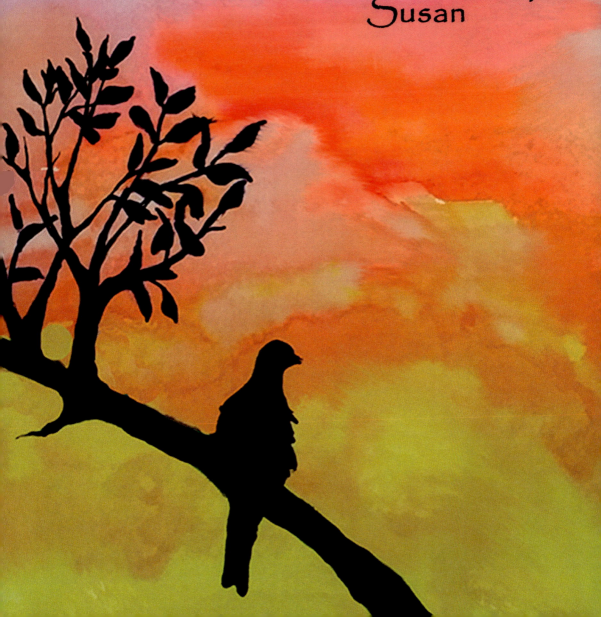

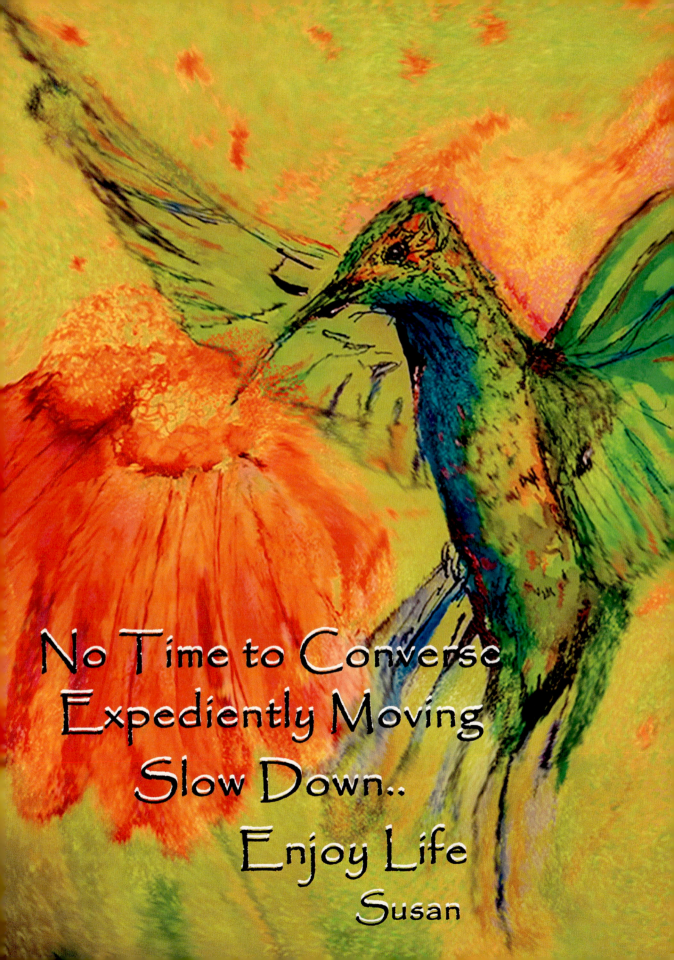

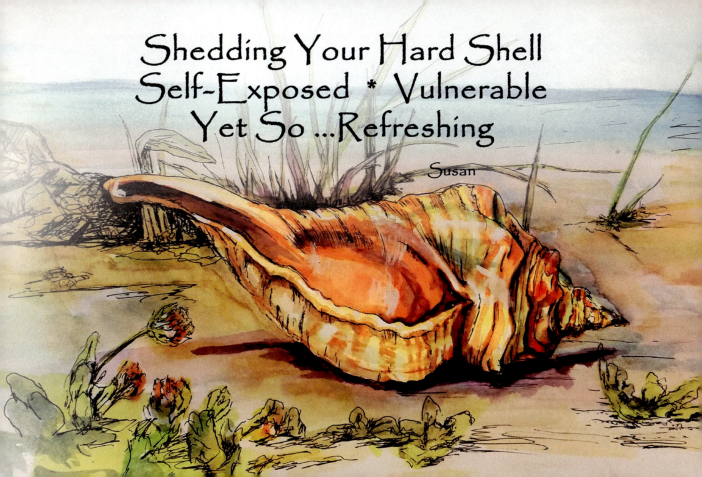

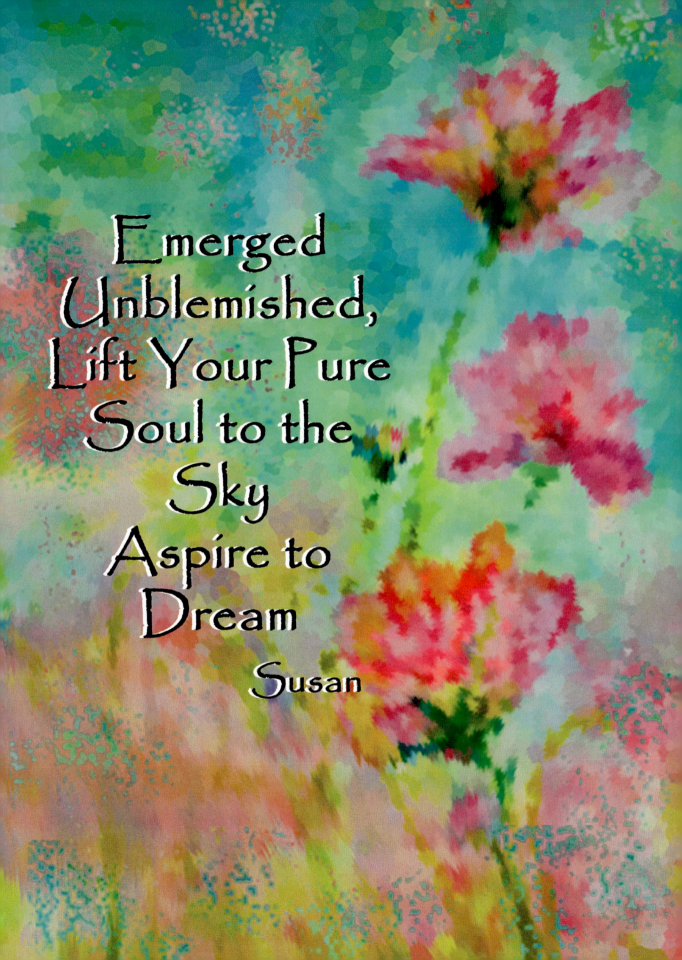

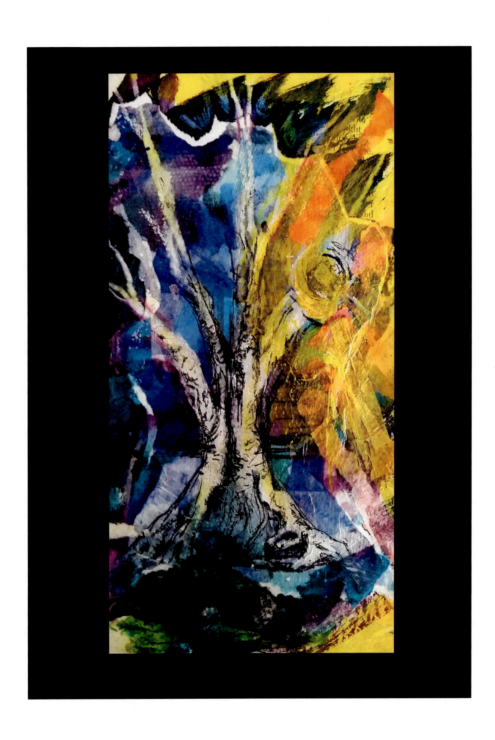

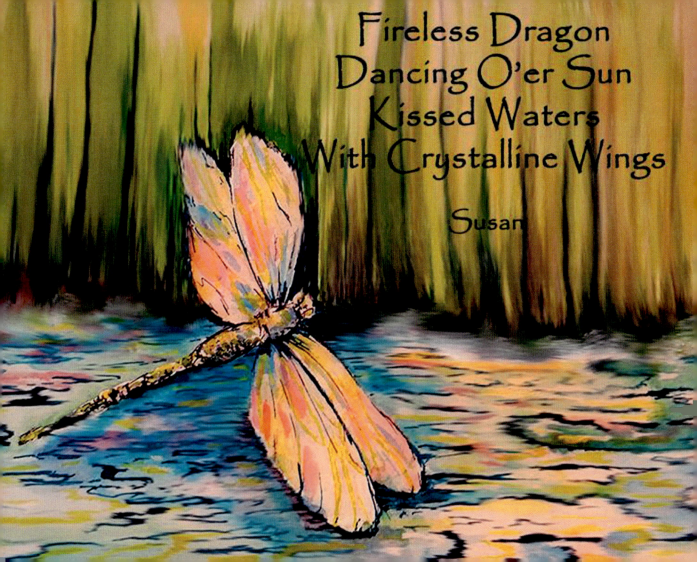

Images Transpose

Ice Particles Suspended

A Few See Castles

Susan

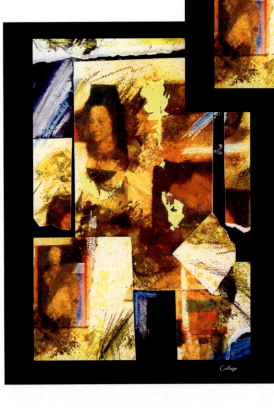

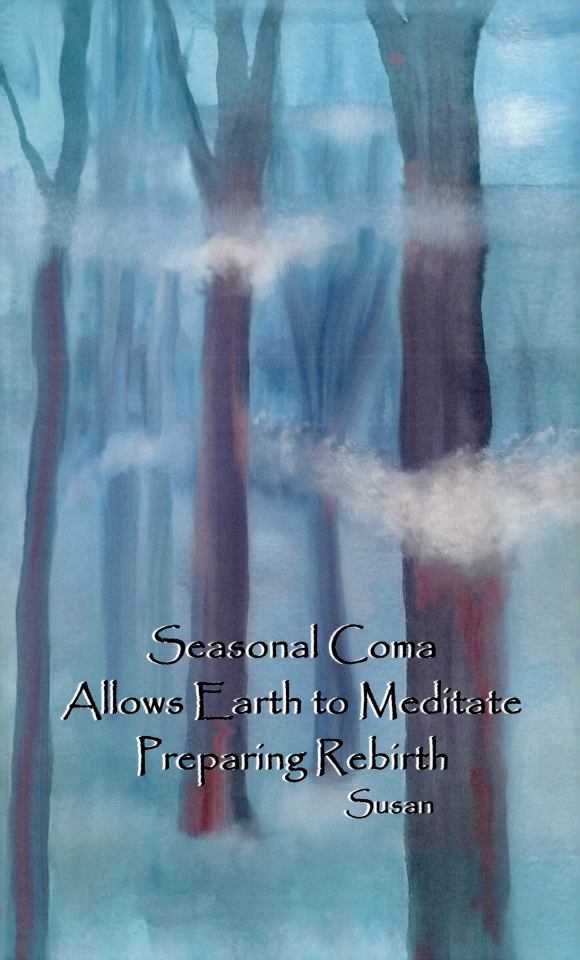

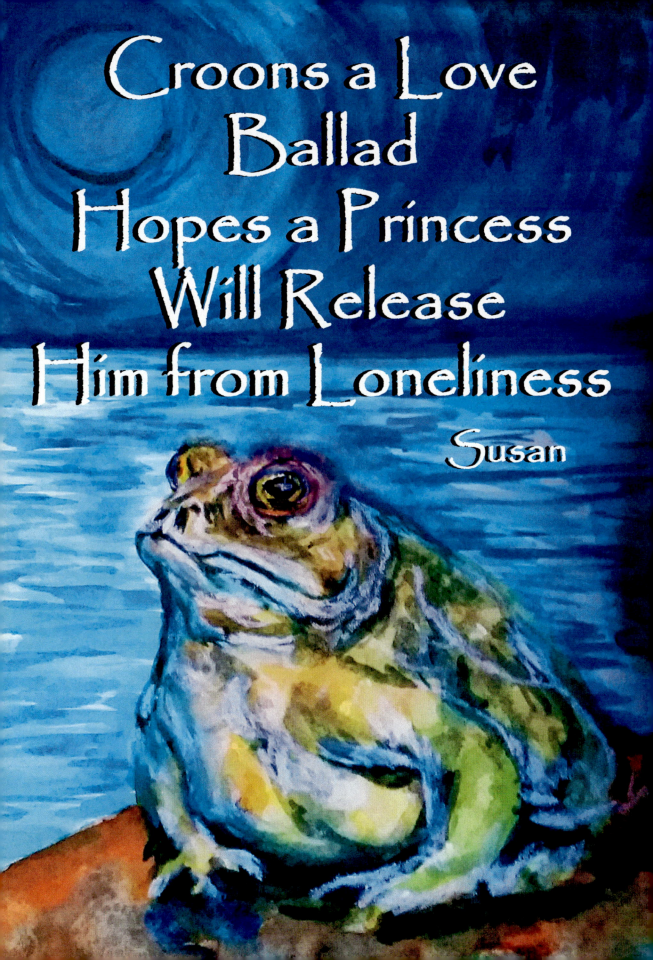

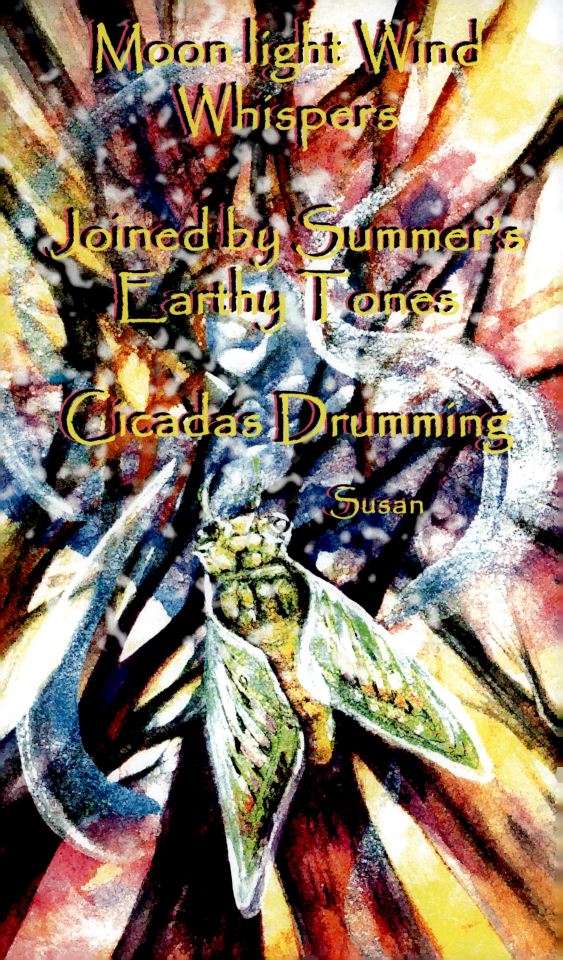

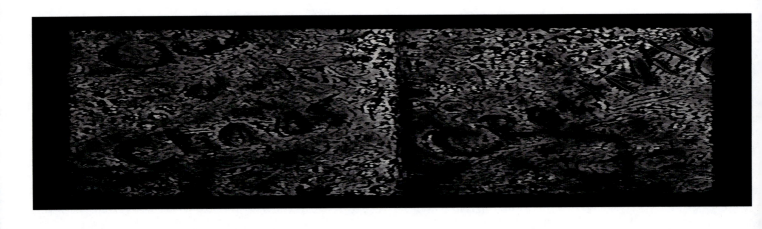

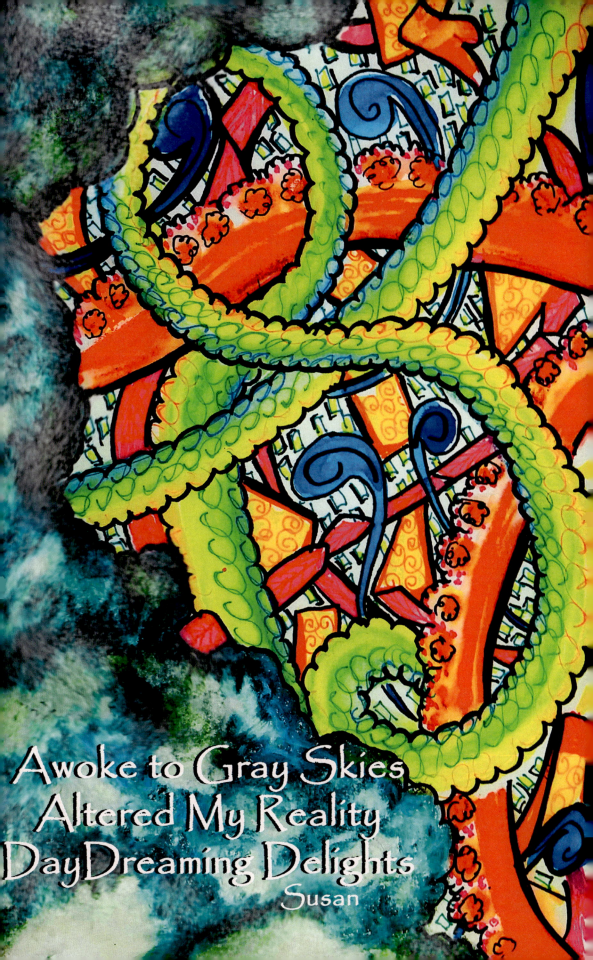

Set Aside Beliefs

You Inhale
My Exhaled Breath

From This Earth
We're One

Susan

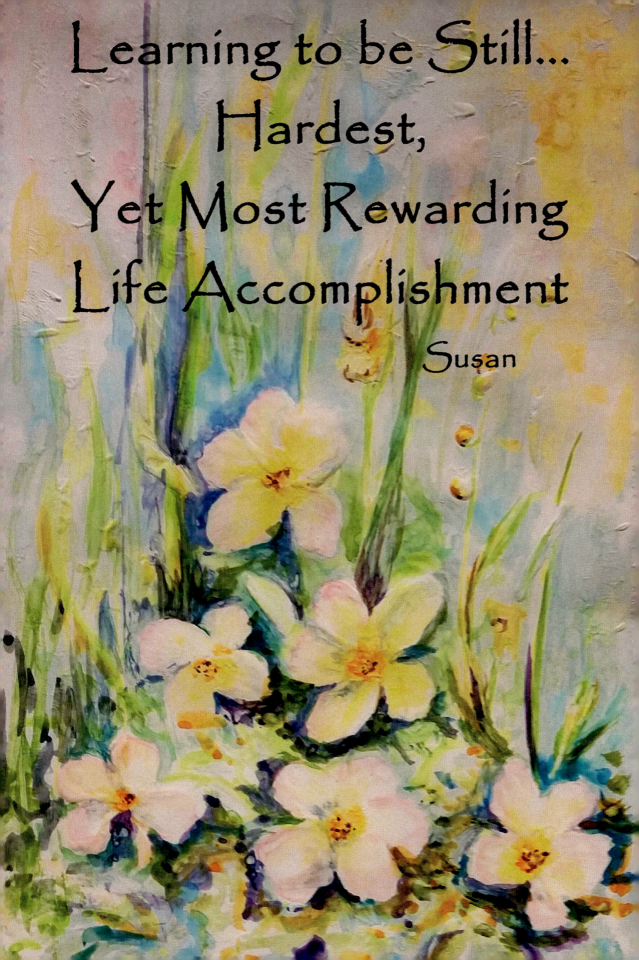

Sun's Final Encore
Casting Spells Across
the Sky
Fire on Water

Susan

Thank you for looking over this collection of my haikus and art work.

I started writing/illustrating a weekly haiku and posting them on Instagram and Facebook. I refer to them as "Monday morning "Hi"ku for you". Monday has had such a bad rap because it seems the majority of the workforce returns on this day. My thought was to bring some joy and beauty back to Monday.

At the request of others, I have put a year and a half of Monday haikus together in this book. I have added some of my sketches/paintings on the opposite pages.

I use a variety of mediums: water color, printmaking, acrylic, color pencils, inks, pastels, fiber, free drawing apps and Adobe PhotoShop

Learning to be still

Susan

Made in the USA
Monee, IL
10 November 2021